The
Little Book of
Revenge

GW00716689

The Little Book of Revenge

Lucrece and Grenville Danvers

Michael O'Mara Humour

First published in Great Britain in 2000 by
Michael O'Mara Books Limited
9 Lion Yard
Tremadoc Road
London SW4 7NQ

A CIP catalogue record for this book is available from the
British Library

ISBN 1-85479-562-7

1 3 5 7 9 1 0 8 6 4 2

Designed and typeset by Design 23
Compiled by Dominique Enright
Printed in China by Leo Paper Products

Lucrece and Grenville Danvers are most grateful to Dominique Enright for her advice and encouragement and for her scholarship and sweet reason in the compilation of this book.

Contents

Revenge
That's one word for it...

getting even • tit for tat • vengeance
retribution • rancour • just deserts
retaliation • resentment • vindictiveness
Nemesis • avengement • sweet revenge
vendetta • death feud • blood for blood
reaction • compensation • payback
keep the wound green • rankle
serve someone • have accounts to settle
unforgiving • an eye for an eye
blood feud • day of reckoning •
punishment

There are many more words and phrases associated with revenge, this very human reaction which demands retaliation for a wrong - **'Revenge is sweet'** crops up time and again all over the world. And some examples of it may be found in this book - from biblical exhortations (**'eye for eye, tooth for tooth'**), to tell-all underpants and tell-all books; from gruesome murders to contradictory words of wisdom; from stink bombs to spiked bread; from pharaohs to hackers. For vengeance comes in many forms - from the pleasure we get in seeing the person who queue-barged us in the express check-out being sent away because they have one too many items in their basket, to the merciless Furies of

Greek myth, unyielding in their pursuit of justice. And then - sometimes just plotting, or fantasizing about, revenge upon someone is enough to melt away feelings of resentment...

Many people enjoy seeing the person who has offended them, or others, come a cropper. They see it as vindication, retribution - a form of justice. Most, however, are not happy to see more extreme forms of revenge: there are still today revenge killings and gang murders; and there are people who choose viciously vindictive ways to revenge themselves (interestingly, these are often people who do not have just grievances, and they themselves invariably land in trouble).

The Roman satirist Juvenal must have been thinking of these people when he wrote, **'Revenge is always the joy of narrow, sick, and petty minds'** (*Satires*). And certainly it is true that vindictiveness leads some 'avengers' to quite ridiculous and petty lengths - often involving damage to property - to vent their feelings. Usually their revenge backfires and they end up in court. So it is not surprising that some people believe that revenge is hollow - **'There is no passion in the human heart that promises so much and pays so little as revenge',** said Josh Billings (the humorist and writer Henry Wheeler Shaw, 1818-85). While others consider that to take revenge is to descend to the level of the one you're taking revenge on. Austin O'Malley felt that **'Revenge is often like biting a dog because the dog bit you'**.

There are also those who believe that the matter should be left to God, to Nemesis, to destiny, to nature, even the law... that the offender will receive due punishment in due course. But, then, as Anthony Trollope remarked in *The Small House At Allington,* **'Those who offend us are generally punished for the offence they give; but we so frequently miss the satisfaction of knowing that we are avenged!'** And it is that satisfaction that we crave.

Just deserts

Perhaps the most famous posthumous act of revenge is that of Tutankhamen, whose tomb allegedly carried an inscription cursing anyone who disturbed it. Shortly after he discovered and began excavating it in 1922/3, the 5th Earl of Carnavon died; the archaeologist Howard Carter was dogged by ill health until his death in 1939 (when, apparently, one of the trumpets found in the tomb was blown for the first time). At the time of Carnavon's death in Cairo, his dog, back in England, also died, while at the same time there was a power failure in Cairo, which was plunged into darkness.

The cause of Lord Carnavon's death was pneumonia, brought on by a bite from a mosquito – the curse, legend has it, read:
> 'Death shall come on swift wings to who disturbs the sleep of the pharaoh.'

Pharaoh's revenge – proverbial nickname for digestive complaint ('Gyppy tummy') suffered by European visitors to Egypt.

In South America, the revenge is Montezuma's.

> Be careful of the words you say,
> Keep them soft and sweet.
> You'll never know from day to day
> Which ones you'll have to eat.
>   Anonymous

Food Additives Adding green or blue food colouring to all items in somebody's refrigerator has been suggested as an apt revenge – perhaps on a person who has consistently slighted the standard of hygiene in your kitchen.

• In 1994, in the States, the ex-wife of an airline pilot, in a fit of vengefulness following their divorce, baked him a loaf of bread laced with marijuana, just before he was due to fly. As she had intended, traces of the drug were found during a random blood test soon after, and he was fired. It took him over two years to clear his name and be reinstated by the airline.

Treacle is sweet, but revenge is sweeter.

J. V. Turner, 1930

• The braggart Pistol – who does not like leeks – has been taunted by Fluellen into eating a leek, ostensibly in revenge for having mocked it when Fluellen wore it in his hat:

> By this leek, I will most horribly revenge. I eat and eat, I swear.
>> William Shakespeare, *King Henry V* (1599)

> Revenge is a luscious fruit which you must leave to ripen.
>> Emile Gaboriau, *File 113* (1867)

It is said that, following their divorce and his remarriage, the first wife of T. S. Eliot, as an act of revenge, went to the trouble of buying the couple a box of chocolates and delivering it to them personally – melted into a sticky mess which she poured through their letter box.

Urban myth?
Dinner to go

A woman whose boyfriend was always late for supper took her revenge when he failed to show up at all for a dinner party. She had been preparing for hours, and a four-course, gourmet meal awaited her guests. All the diners had a great time, despite the empty place at table. When she finally said goodbye to them, she carefully combined all four courses of the absent diner's dinner with a liberal sprinkling of cooking oil into a congealed mess. Covering it with foil, she called a cab and booked the driver (now on double time) to pick up the 'package' and deliver it to her boyfriend's home some eight miles away – cash on delivery. The note on top read 'Enjoy'.

Vengeance is mine... saith the Lord. But is it?

There is some uncertainty as to who should do the revenging – God or man:

> When the Italians hear how God hath reserved vengeance to Himself, they say blasphemously, He knew it was too sweet a bit for man, therefore kept it for His own tooth.
> Samuel Pepys (1633-1703), *Diary*

But God did sometimes recommend that man should take revenge:

> And the Lord said unto Moses, Thus thou shalt say unto the children of Israel ...thou shalt Give life for life, Eye for eye, tooth for tooth, hand for hand, foot for foot, Burning for burning, wound for wound, stripe for stripe.
>
> Exodus 21:23-25

And to Noah he said:

> Whoso sheddeth man's blood, by man shall his blood be shed.
>
> Genesis 9:6

As Israeli occupiers on the West Bank armed themselves in preparation for a spate of revenge killings, in the 1980s, a Western journalist asked one of them whether they didn't feel that it was time to turn the other cheek. The instant response was that that was the *interviewer's* religion – *their* religion advocated eye for eye, tooth for tooth.

The American writer, Oliver Wendell Holmes (1809-94), was of a similar view:

> Wisdom has taught us to be calm
> and meek,
> To take one blow, and turn the other
> cheek;
> It is not written what a man shall do
> If the rude caitiff smite the other too!
>
> 'Non-Resistance' (1861)

• The Soviet statesman, Nikita Khrushchev (1894-1971), had – where the Soviet Union was concerned – no doubts about the matter:

> We had no use for the policies of the Gospels: if someone slaps you, just turn the other cheek. We had shown that anyone who slapped us on the cheek would get his head kicked off.

Yet the Hebrew Bible does not consistently recommend that mankind take revenge:

> O Lord God, to whom vengeance belongeth.

Psalms 94:1

Paradise lost

In Milton's *Paradise Lost* (1667), as far as the Fallen Angels are concerned, vengeance is the order of the day, and they hold a counsel to discuss how to take revenge on God's 'vengeful ire': Moloc (Moloch) suggests that they wage war, however fruitless, against God:
    'which if not victory is yet revenge'.

Belial and Mammon rightly suspect that any action on their part would lead to greater trouble, but the others are hell bent on revenge, and they finally agree on Beelzebub's scheme to tempt man away from God. He assures them:

This would surpass Common revenge.

And so the plot was hatched:
The infernal serpent; he it was,
whose guile,
Stirr'd up with envy and revenge,
deceiv'd
the mother of mankind.

As he insinuated himself into the body of the coiled-up serpent, Satan already had an inkling that this revenge might not work out:

Revenge at first thought sweet,
Bitter ere long back on itself recoils.
John Milton (1608-74), *Paradise Lost*

He was right – retribution was swift to follow:

And the Lord God said unto the serpent,
Because thou has done this, thou art cursed above all cattle, and above every beast of the field; upon thy belly shalt thou go, and dust shalt thou eat all the days of thy life.

And I will put enmity between thee and
the woman, and between thy seed and
her seed; it shall bruise thy head,
and thou shalt bruise his heel.

Genesis 3:13-15

Adam thought this was a good idea:
. . . to crush his head
would be revenge indeed.

John Milton, *Paradise Lost*

And mankind has continued to kill snakes,
though anybody claiming that they have
killed a snake in revenge for the serpent's
act of treachery in the Garden of Eden
would get a few odd looks.

The biter bit...
dumb animals?

The *New Scientist* reports a 'bizarre form of posthumous revenge' from rattlesnakes. Up to an hour after death a rattlesnake can lunge and snap at a moving object, and a number of people have been attacked by snakes they have killed. One man, having shot a rattlesnake, decapitated it and waited five minutes before picking up the head. As he did so, it twisted round and sank its teeth into his hand. In surprised pain, he grasped his finger with the other hand, which the bodiless rattler promptly bit as well.

Another rare instance of animals taking deliberate revenge was reported in a Saudi Arabian newspaper: a man driving to work one morning ran into a group of monkeys on the road, killing one of them. Its companions chased furiously after the car but couldn't catch up with it. Driving home that evening, the man saw the monkeys still on the road, gathered round the dead one, and as he approached, they threw themselves on the car, chittering furiously and scrabbling at the windows. The man had to shake them off his car by accelerating hard.

In the Far East a circus elephant had to
be destroyed for taking revenge on a
youth who had fed her a banana with a
chilli hidden inside it. When he returned
to see the elephants an hour or so later,
she recognized him, knocked him to the
ground, and crushed him to death.

In West Bengal a group of elephants
rampaged through a village causing
considerable damage. One villager,
whose house was wrecked, managed to
catch a baby elephant and in retaliation
killed it. Later, its mother returned to his
home and trampled him to death.

Saki (H. H. Munro), best-known for his short stories, often used animals to satirize aspects of society that he disliked, or as agents of revenge. The cat, Tobermory, for instance, learns to talk (in English) and, having been in the position to overhear a great deal is only too prepared to be indiscreet at a house party, much to the discomfiture of all.

The poet John Skelton (?1460-1529) in 'Philip Sparrow' calls for a moderate revenge upon cats, following the death of a pet sparrow:

> Vengeance I ask and cry,
> By way of exclamation,
> On the whole nation
> Of cats wild and tame:
> God send them sorrow and shame!

Hell hath no fury...

For some reason, women are considered (by men) to be the more vengeful of the sexes. Perhaps they have more cause.

'Sweet is revenge – especially to women.'
George Gordon, Lord Byron
(1788-1824), *Don Juan* (1819-24)

A woman always has her revenge ready.
Moliére (Jean-Baptiste Coquelin; 1622-73),
Tartuffe (1669)

No one delights more in vengeance than a woman.
Juvenal (AD 60-130), *Satires,* XIII

• The written word seems to be a popular means of revenge among women – recognizing the power of words – though it is not the only way they choose. What distinguishes their methods of revenge, is that they are all imaginative, but do not inflict physical injury.

• A Bristol woman, when she found out that the man she had met through a dating agency – and who she said had plied her with chocolates and flowers and asked her to marry him – was not divorced as she had understood him to be, sewed labels on his underpants, wrote LYING BASTARD on the labels, bundled all his clothes together and delivered them to his wife.

Urban Myth?
Wheeler dealer
A woman who was estranged from her husband was so angry at his unreasonable behaviour that she decided to get her own back. She sold the Mercedes they had previously shared for the princely sum of £1.

Urban Myth?
It all adds up
A woman left home in fury at her partner's behaviour. She returned while he was away on a long business trip, made a call to the Speaking Clock in New York and left the handset off.

Urban Myth?
Scissor happy
A wife found out that her husband was unfaithful, and cut up his expensive suits into neat strips.

Urban Myth?
Empty life
A wife put her wine-connoisseur husband's entire collection of vintage wines out on neighbours' doorsteps, adding a bottle of wine to their usual milk order.

Urban Myth?
Something fishy

A woman who had been jilted by her lover, used her key to enter his flat when he was away on a long business trip. She took with her two pints of peeled prawns. Slipping the curtains off their rings, she carefully threaded the prawns at even intervals into the heading. She re-hung the curtains, turned up the central heating thermostat and left. It took him days to track down the source of the terrible stench of rotting fish, and months to get rid of it.

Making public a person's misdemeanours, crimes or sins is a popular way of taking revenge on that person (assuming one is not libelling or slandering them in any way) – that the world knows all about the offender's misdeeds is often adequate compensation; if it should block that person's plans and hopes, so much the better. This form of vengeance-taking is particularly effective if the person is a public figure, though some of these figures have a way of bouncing back.

• Following the public revelation of the Foreign Secretary Robin Cook's extra-marital affair, which led to his divorce and, later, his marriage to his lover – who, his first wife, Margaret, claimed, he felt 'would have made life very difficult for him' if he had ended their relationship – Margaret Cook published her book, *A Slight and Delicate Creature*, retailing her unhappy marriage to a serially unfaithful husband (in which she also made clear how unsuited he would be to such a position as Prime Minister). Its serialization in a major newspaper made sure that aspects of his life that he'd probably rather have kept private

were very much in the public eye –
though how much lasting damage it did
is uncertain. Mrs Cook later insisted that
she wrote the book 'for herself', not out
of a desire for revenge.

• An acquaintance of English MP Steven Norris, whose husband had left her at the same time as his friend Mr Norris left his wife, saw her opportunity to take revenge on errant men in general, and on Mr Norris in particular, whom she seemed to hold to blame for her husband's action, by writing to the Conservative Party about Steven Norris's infidelities and his unsuitability for the position of Mayor of London. Her triumph when he was dropped as mayoral candidate, was, however, short-lived: he was reinstated only days later.

The female of the species is more deadly...?

In revenge and in love, woman is more barbarous than man.
Friedrich Nietzsche (1844-1900), *Beyond Good and Evil* (1886)

The avenging deities in Greek mythology were women – the Erinyes or Furies, terrifying of aspect, with writhing serpents for hair, blood dripping from their eyes – who relentlessly pursued and tormented those they judged to have done wrong. But, unyielding as they were, they were acting objectively in the cause of justice, pure and simple, if merciless.

The sorceress Medea, famous for her ruthlessness and revengeful nature, was, however, motivated by personal enmity. Because she had fallen in love with Jason, she took revenge on his uncle Pelias for the murder of Jason's parents. Having displayed to Pelias's daughters how she could restore an old sheep to capering lambhood by cutting it up, boiling it, and then uttering a charm, she told them she could do likewise for their elderly father and persuaded them to chop the old man up when he was in a drugged sleep and throw the pieces into a boiling cauldron. She then left without a word.

Years later, she took revenge on the daughter of King Creon, with whom Jason had fallen in love, by sending her a poisoned cloak, which killed her. Then – a somewhat extreme person – fearing that King Creon would avenge his daughter's death on her sons, she spared him the trouble and killed them herself. This earned her the fury of Jason, from whom she fled to Athens, where she eventually got herself into more trouble and departed for Asia.

This behaviour would surely not have come into Sir Thomas Browne's category of 'feminine':

> Since women do most delight in revenge, it may seem but feminine manhood to be vindictive.
>
> Sir Thomas Browne (1605-82),
> *Christian Morals* (1716)

Payback time?

Men tend to be more physically destructive when it comes to revenge; perhaps they would be better to follow this advice.

> When a man steals your wife, there is no better revenge than to let him keep her.
>> Sacha Guitry (1885-1957), *Elle et toi*

• In a recent case of revenge in California, the woman is clearly better off without the man. When she jilted him he took a nasty revenge by claiming on the Internet that he was a woman interested in enacting violent sexual fantasies – and then gave his ex-girlfriend's address to all the men who replied.

• In Wales, another jilted man took a less vicious, but nevertheless unpleasant, revenge on his former lover by painting with white undercoat and red gloss paint twenty pairs of her shoes, as well as splattering with paint and bleach twenty-seven shirts, eight jerseys and three sweatshirts belonging to her. (He had to pay compensation.)

• When a Pembrokeshire guesthouse owner found his wife in bed with one of their regular customers, he too took his revenge on clothes: he stormed into the man's room, took up all the many bags of clothing he found – which included handmade Italian suits – and threw the lot into a cesspit.

Urban Myth?
Call girl

A London man jilted by his girlfriend had cards printed, including a voluptuous photograph and advertising no-holds-barred sex. The phone number was that of his ex-girlfriend. He then spent several happy hours posting them up in the Central London telephone boxes where prostitutes advertise.

Urban Myth?
The grass is greener

When a keen gardener and middle-aged husband discovered his wife's infidelity, he waited until she went away to 'visit her sister' then packed his lawn mower and all his possessions – except his watering can – into the family car.

Before he drove off into the night, he sprinkled fast-growing lawn seed over the carpets and soft furnishings, paying special attention to the marital bed. He then watered the seed liberally and locked up the house. When his errant wife returned the house was covered in a sparse green growth of grass.

When good love turns bad!

1 Send an ex-boyfriend or girlfriend a dozen long-stemmed roses – all dead.

2 Put an ad in a 'lonely hearts' column on his/her behalf giving his/her address.

3 Call ten double-glazing or financial services companies and pretend that he/she would welcome their calls – giving his/her phone number.

4 Place an ad in the classified section of a newspaper putting his/her house up for sale. Add 'callers welcome'.

5 Sew a little lace around the shorts or jockstrap of a boyfriend who expects his washing to be done, and pack it carefully in his bag so that he discovers it only when he goes to change – in public!

Blood for blood

Perhaps the most barbarous act of revenge
in Greek mythology was committed by a
man, the king Atreus, who, when he
learned that his brother Thyestes had
seduced his wife, murdered Thyestes' sons
and served them to him in a banquet.
When the unsuspecting Thyestes had eaten,
Atreus had the children's heads brought in
on a platter. Thyestes' own revenge for this
gruesome act was to put on the house of
Atreus a curse, which led to a number of
bloody killings, culminating in Orestes'
murder of his mother, Clytemnestra and her
lover, Aegisthus, in revenge for their murder
of his father, Agamemnon.

• The house of Atreus was a dynasty in which this saying would have had no place:

> Blood cannot be washed out with blood.
>
> > Persian proverb

More commonly, it was – still is? – believed that blood can wash out blood.

> For a deadly blow let him pay with a deadly blow: it is for him who has done a deed to suffer.
>
> > Aeschylus (c.525–c.456 BC), *The Libation Bearers*

• The ancient Greeks were clearly in the 'eye-for-eye' type of justice camp.

> Men regard it as their right to return evil for evil – and if they cannot, feel they have lost their liberty.
> Aristotle (384-322 BC), *Nicomachean Ethics*

> This is sweet: to see your foe
> Perish and pay to justice all he owes.
> Euripides (*c.*480-*c.*406 BC), *Heracles*

While Euripides and the other Ancients see revenge purely as justice, for Shakespeare's Richard, Duke of Gloucester, it is also a way of lessening grief – or so he claims, though he is ambitious and has no qualms in using murder and treachery to get what he wants, which is the throne, and which he ultimately ascends as Richard III. Here he swears revenge for the murder of his father.

> To weep is to make less the depth of grief;
> Tears, then for babes – blows and revenge for me!
>
> William Shakespeare, *King Henry VI,*
> Part 3 (1595)

Others of Shakespeare's characters seem to be even less justly motivated ... in a play full of vengeance and murders, Aaron the Moor, lover of Tamora, queen of the Goths, anticipates the murder he gets Tamora's sons to commit. (In an act reminiscent of Atreus's, Titus later murders Tamora's sons and serves them up in a pie, some of which Tamora eats.)

> Vengeance is in my heart, death in my hand,
> Blood and revenge are hammering in my head.

William Shakespeare, *Titus Andronicus* (*c.*1590)

While the revenge he envisaged was nearly as bloody, one can feel some sympathy for Shylock, in that he had a genuine grievance. Asked why he wants his pound of flesh – and he means it literally – Shylock tries to justify his desire for revenge in an impassioned speech:

> ...if it will feed nothing else, it will feed my revenge. He hath disgraced me, and hindered me half a million; laughed at my losses, mocked at my gains, scorned my nation, thwarted my bargains, cooled my friends, heated mine enemies; and what's his reason? I am a Jew.
>
> ...If you prick us, do we not bleed?

If you tickle us, do we not laugh? If you poison us, do we not die? And if you wrong us, shall we not revenge? If we are like you in the rest, we will resemble you in that.

William Shakespeare, *The Merchant of Venice* (1596-8)

Publish and damn

His pen is breathing revenge.
Leo Tolstoy, *Vaska Shibanov* (1855-65)

For writers of fiction, there is a
particularly satisfying way to take
revenge – which is to base the
characters in their novels or short stories
on people who have distressed or
offended them in some way. (Obviously,
some caution has to be exercised to
avoid charges of libel.)

As a child, the writer Saki (H. H. Munro) was brought up by two aunts who were perhaps more concerned for his moral welfare than for his happiness, and the character of ten-year-old Conradin in the story *Sredni Vashtar* must surely be based on himself.

Brought up by a much older cousin, whom 'he hated with a desperate sincerity', Conradin devotes himself to Sredni Vashtar, a large polecat ferret which he both fears and worships as a god. 'Do one thing for me, Sredni Vashtar,' he prays over and over. When his cousin goes to the shed (having disposed of a hen Conradin used to keep there) to see why the boy is still visiting it, he chants his hymn:

Sredni Vashtar went forth,
His thoughts were red thoughts and his teeth were white.
His enemies called for peace, but he brought them death, Sredni Vashtar the Beautiful.

After watching from the window for some time, Conradin sees to his satisfaction the ferret slipping out of the shed, dark wet stains about its jaws and throat.

• In 1996 the press had a bit of fun with the news of the forthcoming publication of a thriller by the former MP, Timothy Renton, seeing in it an act of revenge on his wife who had recently published her first novel, *Winter Butterfly,* in which one of the characters is a dishonest, philandering MP. Mr Renton's novel features a politician's wife who is addicted to gambling and sinks into debt.

Don't get mad, get even

It is difficult to fight against anger; for a man will buy revenge with his soul.

Heraclitus (*c.*540-*c.*480 BC)

The workplace is a breeding ground for feelings of resentment, as well as for little Napoleons, some of whom have to be taken down a peg or two to make life supportable for the others.

• A man who had for some years been working in the service department of a firm in Wales was ignored when he applied for a new position that had just been created in the firm. He resigned in protest, and on his last afternoon he destroyed all of the test rigs he had built, and the notes he had made to speed up the job. To his satisfaction he later heard that three members of staff were needed to do his old job.

Urban myth?
How about a compromise?

When a group of office workers in Kansas, whose boss was 'always on a power trip, and completely intolerable as a supervisor', heard of an imminent visit from a couple of corporate executives from New York, they saw their chance for revenge. As the hated supervisor showed their guests (both women) around he was unaware of the surprise awaiting him in his office: two nude prostitutes in a compromising position. The next they heard of their boss was that he was no longer employed there.

• A computer genius with a grudge against his former employers whom he felt, wrongly as it happens, had treated him unreasonably in reprimanding him for working against their interests, used his keyboard skills to hack into a mobile-phone network and trick thousands of mobile-phone users in to telephoning the company, blocking its switchboard for days. At the same time he let loose a 'Trojan Horse' virus into the computer systems of companies in the same business as his erstwhile employers.

Hacking can be a means of wreaking vengeance, but it is rare that it is at the root of the revenge taking, as here.

• A company issued a challenge on the Internet to hackers, defying them to break into a computer network protected by their 'firewall' security system, Access Denied. Even hackers who could crack military, government, commercial and private systems with relative ease and speed had still not breached the firewall after spending several weeks and making 240,000 attacks on it. Piqued by his failure, a particularly vindictive hacker – who felt he had been made to look a fool, having boasted to his friends that he could do it in five minutes – instead hacked into the financial records of the creator of Access Denied, and added six default notices and a County Court judgement to them, causing the man all manner of problems.

Urban myth?
A step up

A woman in the US was working as a temp, at a major insurance company. Her boss who was very conceited and vain about her appearance, treated her like rubbish. One day the employee was sitting across from her superior in a big, important meeting, taking notes. The boss always slipped off her shoes at these meetings. The temp. secretly reached over with her foot and dragged one shoe to her side of the table. Soon the boss had to go to the front of the room for her presentation. She could only find one shoe. She was frantic. Everyone laughed at her and she got the nickname: 'one-shoe Sue', which she HATED!

Urban Myth?
Undercover agent

A bank cashier suffered under a change in management, and considered the new manager to be a complete idiot. The cashier was then fired for asking to be excused a staff meeting to take a final exam. He went straight to a magazine stand and collected a huge batch of subscription cards to magazines, from 'adult' titles to arts and crafts, and took out subscriptions in the manager's name to nearly a hundred periodicals.

Urban Myth?
As you sew...
A shop assistant took a novel revenge on her unreasonable boss. She unpicked the seam in his coat and inserted one of those shoplifting security disks. She neatly sewed the seam back up and every time the boss went out of the door with his coat on, he set off the shoplifting alarm. He never worked out why.

Urban myth?
We're through

A skilled worker in the sweet factory of a British seaside town was made redundant after a long and hardworking life at the 'rockface'. Before he left he carefully prepared a mile of sweet rock which should have read 'A Present from B*******L' all the way through. Instead the hundreds of sticks of rock that found their way to the kiosks on the prom. read 'F**k off!'

Urban myth?
The good seed and the bad

A disgruntled farmworker was sick to death of being sent out day after day to plough acres of farmland in straight rows. The very demanding farmer had made him re-plough one particular field, on the slopes of a valley, three times. As the sun set on the rich brown earth that evening, walkers were surprised to read 'Farmer B**** is Sh*t ploughed in perfect 12-foot letters.

• In a puerile act of revenge after his airline reservations twice went wrong in 1998, a former senior New York City official let off stink bombs on two TWA flights between New York and France, on one of these occasions actually forcing the aircraft to make an unscheduled landing, so appalling was the stench.

A Mafia clan in Sicily recently took a grisly revenge for the loss of useful pay-offs in the 'racket of the loved one', which brings in money from burials. When the Mayor of Catania, to rid the cemetery of mob influence, brought in an outside manager to run it, the gangsters switched the recently deceased between coffins just before their funerals, to the horror of the bereaved families.

Crime and punishment

Revenge is a kind of wild justice, which the more man's nature runs to, the more ought law to weed it out.

> Francis Bacon (1561-1626), 'Of Revenge', *Essays* (1625)

As the law evolved from a system, often ritualized, of tribal or communal avengement, it comes as no surprise that the law courts are full of people out to take revenge upon others. However, one might feel that those whose occupation is to see that the law is carried out would be above petty acts of revenge.

• In 1997, Fulham police at last caught on camera the person who had for some two years been repeatedly scratching a couple's cars. It was a neighbour of theirs, a barrister (and son of a Law Lord), who had been creeping out at night to scrape at the paintwork of the Porsche and Range Rover. In court he admitted that 'it was for revenge', following a dispute over a parking space.

• Those who have a cynical view of the law will recognize how vengeful is the Irish curse:

> May you have a lawsuit in which you know you are in the right.

• One has to admire the calm tone of this aggrieved millionaire:

Gentlemen:
You have undertaken to ruin me. I will not sue you, for law takes too long. I will ruin you.
Sincerely,
    Cornelius Vanderbilt (1794-1877), letter to his business associates

• Equally direct was the owner of a sex shop in Rouen, who took revenge for a bounced cheque by displaying the offender's name and address in his window.

Heaping coals of fire

Second thoughts?

St Paul is not recommending literally pouring hot coals on someone's head; rather, he is saying 'avenge not yourselves' (Romans 12:19) – the Lord will take care of that...

That this is how to be avenged: Therefore, if thine enemy hunger, feed him; if he thirst, give him drink: for in so doing thou shalt heap coals of fire on his head.

Romans 12:20

• In the seventeenth century J. Clark also thought it best not to take action, writing in his *Paroemiologia Anglo-Latina* (1639):
'To forget a wrong is best revenge.'

• Joseph Patrick Kennedy (or it might have been his son, Robert F. Kennedy, or perhaps another US politician, Everett Dirksen) did not think people should not take revenge – but he advocated keeping one's temper:
'Don't get mad, get even.'

• Francis Bacon (1561-1626) did not think getting even had any merit:
In taking revenge, a man is but even with his enemy; but in passing it over, he is superior.
'Of Revenge', *Essays* (1625)

• No revenge is more honourable than the one not taken.

Spanish proverb

• Recompense to no man evil for evil.

Romans 12:17

• Even the Mafia, it would seem, can have their doubts:

> Vito Corleone: You talk about *vengeance*. Is *vengeance* going to bring your son back to you? Or my boy to me?
>
> Mario Puzo, *The Godfather* (1969)

• Leon Trotsky (1879-1940), writing about his arch-enemy, Stalin, thought matters of revenge were best left to history:

> The vengeance of history is more terrible than the vengeance of the most powerful General Secretary.

• Francis Bacon again:

> A man that studieth revenge keeps his own wounds green, which otherwise would heal and do well.

'On Revenge', *Essays* (1625)

• Common sense overrides the old proverb 'Revenge is sweet':

> Revenge is sweet... but not when you're on the receiving end.

> Revenge is sweet... to think about, but stupid to do.
>> Later qualifications, probably US

• Living well is the best revenge.

• The best revenge is to live long enough to be a problem to your children.
> Proverb

• ...and thus the whirligig of time brings in his revenges.
William Shakespeare, *Twelfth Night* (1601)

Revenge on the silver screen

Revenge: 'crude melodrama' (*Halliwell's Film Guide*)

Revenge (*Blood Feud*):
    a vengeful Sicilian woman

Revenge: 'brutal, shallow thriller' (*Halliwell*)

Revenge at El Paso (*Ace High*):
    spaghetti Western

Revenge of Billy the Kid: 'Amateurish horror spook' (*Sight and Sound*)

The Revenge of Frankenstein

Revenge of the Dead (*Night of the Ghouls*)

Revenge of the Gladiators (*Fire over Rome*)

The Revenge of the Pink Panther: incompetent Inspector Clouseau strikes again

Revenge of the Vampires (*Mask of Satan*): vengeance 200 years after the event

Revenge of the Zombies: 'Unpersuasive horror cheapie' (*Halliwell*)

The Revengers (Western)

Theatre of Blood: an actor takes revenge on his critics

Vengeance: a brain seeks revenge on his body's murderer

The Vengeance of Fu Manchu: revenge against Interpol

The Vengeance of She: 'Grotesquely unpersuasive reincarnation melodrama' (*Halliwell*)

Mask of the Avenger: a count's son avenges his father's death

The Avenging Boxer: Hong Kong martial arts

Retribution: a vengeful (dead) murderer

Sound biteback

Revenge (Eurythmics, 1986)

Revenge (Bill Cosby, 1967)

Revenge (Original Soundtrack, 1995)

Revenge (James Dead, 1999)

Revenge (Kiss, 1992)

Revenge (Alastis, 1998)

Revenge (Janis Ian, 1995)

Revenge (TSOL)

Revenge (John Stewart)

Make Them Die Slowly (White Zombie, 1989)

Still Climbing (Brownstone, 1997)

Sweet Revenge (Generation X, 1998)

Revenge on the Telemarketers...
(Tom Mabe, 2000)

Revenge of the Nerds (Original Soundtrack)

Revenge of the Underdog
(Singers & Players)

Revenge of the Goldfish (Inspiral Carpets,
1992)

Michael O'Mara Humour

Other 'Little Book' titles published by
Michael O'Mara Books Ltd:

The Little Book of Farting – ISBN 1-85479-445-0
The Little Book of Stupid Men – ISBN 1-85479-454-X
The Little Toilet Book – ISBN 1-85479-456-6
The Little Book of Venom – ISBN 1-85479-446-9
The Little Book of Pants – ISBN 1-85479-477-9
The Little Book of Pants 2 – ISBN 1-85479-557-0
The Little Book of Bums – ISBN 1-85479-561-9
The Little Book of Voodoo – ISBN 1-85479-560-0
The Little Book of Blondes – ISBN 1-85479-558-9
The Little Book of Magical Love Spells – ISBN 1-85479-559-7

If you would like more information, please contact our
UK Sales Department:

    fax 020 7 622 6956

    e-mail:jokes@michaelomarabooks.com